HEADSTART HISTO

The Anglo Norman Church

by

Christopher Harper-Bill

HEADSTART HISTORY

Published by   HEADSTART HISTORY
                      PO Box 41, Bangor, Gwynedd, LL57 1SB

Set by   C.B.S.
                      155 Hamilton Road,
                      Felixstowe, Suffolk, IP11 7DR

Printed by   DOTESIOS LTD
                      Kennet House, Kennet Way,
                      Trowbridge, Wiltshire BA14 8RN

ISBN   1 873041 90 X

A CIP catalogue record for this book is available from the British Library.

CONTENTS

Frontispiece :   William I in an initial of Norman
                    inspiration: *Chronicle of Battle
                    Abbey*. Early 12th century
                    BL, MS Cotton, Domitian A.11,
                    f21

INTRODUCTION

The HEADSTART HISTORY PAPERS aim to identify important themes and topics the significance of which extends beyond
the studies of professional historians. The PAPERS are distilla-
tions of the research of distinguished scholars in a form appro-
priate to students and the general reader.

Christopher Harper-Bill studied at King's College, London
under the late R. Allen Brown who has been a great influence on
his intellectual development and who he succeeded as General
Editor of the *Suffolk Charters* series of the Suffolk Record
Society. Dr. Harper-Bill is also General Editor of the *Studies in
the History of Medieval Religion*, and is joint editor with his
wife, Dr. Ruth Harvey, of *The Ideals and Practice of Medieval
Knighthood: Proceedings of the Strawberry Hill Conferences*.

Dr. Harper-Bill's main interests are medieval ecclesiastical
records and the social history of religion and his publications to
date illustrate how well qualified he is to write this **PAPER** on
the Anglo-Norman Church. He traces a path through the relationship between the crown, the English church and the papacy:
the impact of the Hildebrandine reforms with its challenge of
moral renewal running parallel with the struggle over lay
investiture. We are shown how the Normans had developed 'a
theology of armed action' which they took to the Mediterranean
lands and how they used the church as an 'agent of colonisation'
in England. As archbishops both Lanfranc and Anselm are seen
as 'uncompromising Gregorians' and under the latter we see the
first appearance in England of the conflict between *regnum* and
sacerdotum - a conflict which was a dominant theme in Western
Christendom.

This **PAPER** covers an important and fascinating period in the
English Church and Christopher Harper-Bill has provided us

with a lucid explanation of the intricate problems which challenged the Anglo-Norman church and state.

It is always a pleasure to thank an author for support and Christopher Harper-Bill has been unstinting in his support for MEDIEVAL HISTORY indeed for all HEADSTART HISTORY's activities. Like all my authors he has a distinguished record of publication as well as an unselfish enthusiasm for his pupils and that interest in his teaching is shown in his dedication.

Judith Loades
Bangor, 1992

For the students of medieval history at
St. Mary's College, Twickenham
who always manage to make life fun.

The Papal Revolution

The history of the church in England in the late eleventh and early twelfth centuries was deeply influenced by the aftermath of two revolutionary events. The Norman Conquest was no less dramatic in its impact on ecclesiastical life than in the changes which it wrought in secular society.[1] The church, like the land, was under new management, and the new French elite introduced important organisational changes based on continental models. Even more significant than the Norman take-over of the Old English church, however, was the rise to power at Rome of a radical group who shattered age-old concepts of the relationship of religion and government within Christian society. This movement is known to historians as the papal reform, or the Gregorian or Hildebrandine reform, after its most dramatic exponent, the archdeacon Hildebrand, who from 1073 to 1085 pontificated over the western church as Pope Gregory VII.[2]

The reform movement at Rome falls into two distinct phases. From 1046 to 1057 the emphasis was placed on moral renewal. A succession of German popes, of whom the greatest was Leo IX (1049-54), with the full cooperation of the Emperor Henry III, mounted a determined attack on those clergy who had fallen from the ideals of

---

1 R.A. Brown, *The Normans and the Norman Conquest*, 2nd edn, Woodbridge 1985, 216-25.

2 For a most stimulating interpretation, see still G. Tellenbach, *Church, State and Christian Society at the time of the Investiture Controversy*, Oxford 1940; most conveniently, see H.E.J. Cowdrey, 'Pope Gregory VII', *Medieval History* I i, 1991, 23-37.

the early church. The twin evils which they sought to
eradicate were simony, or the purchase of ecclesiastical
office from patrons, and nicolaitism, the keeping of wives,
or in reforming eyes mistresses, by priests. Simony was
regarded by hard-liners at Rome as heretical, for it in-
volved trading in the gift of the Holy Spirit. The squalor
of sexual relations could not be tolerated in those who
celebrated the sacrament of the altar. Clerical marriage,
moreover, created the likelihood of an hereditary priestly
caste, passing on churches and bishoprics from father to
son as family possessions. The papal reform movement
was an attempt to recover the purity of the primitive
church. It offended a great many vested interest, but it
is remarkable how quickly its basic premises came to be
accepted by Western Christendom. Neither cash transactions to acquire churches nor the keeping of women
by priests ceased overnight, but from the end of the
eleventh century both activities became something to be
hidden, a lapse from a newly-accepted norm. To take
two English examples, in 1091 Herbert Losinga pur-
chased the bishopric of East Anglia from William Rufus,
but soon became troubled by the grave moral danger
which he had incurred and, to the king's fury, surrendered his see into the hands of the pope who, recognising his merits, reinstated him.[3] Herbert, who proved to
be an excellent bishop, had suddenly come to terms with
a reforming ideology which was an innovation in his
own lifetime. Around 1100 it was common form for the
rich prebendal churches of St. Paul's cathedral in Lon-

---

3 C. Harper-Bill, ed., *English Episcopal Acta vi: Norwich 1070-
1214*, 1990, xxix.

don to pass from father to son; by 1150 it was extremely rare and noteworthy when such succession occurred.[4]

Within a decade of the Norman Conquest, however, the emphasis of the papal reform movement had shifted. Speculative theology combined with practical political considerations to convince the Roman reformers that the root cause of all evil within the church was lay domination of the clergy. Just as the local lord, whose ancestor had built a church on his estate, claimed much of its revenue and the right to appoint its priest, so at the highest level the king distributed bishoprics and abbeys to men who had given him good service and would continue to do so. In practical terms this might be seen as a sensible and just arrangement. The church held a high proportion of the landed wealth of Western Europe (some 25% in England, according to Domesday Book), and in return for this provided, in effect, the salaries of those educated men whose service was ever more essential in a world where written government was becoming increasingly the norm. In the first flush of enthusiasm in Rome, however, such practical considerations were forgotten. Gregory VII and his circle convinced themselves that if lay control of the church could be broken, moral reform would present no problem. The pope fulminated continually against investiture by the king of bishops and abbots with ring and staff, the badges of their spiritual office; but in fact investiture was only a symbol. What the reformers rejected was selection of the church's

---

4 C.N.L. Brooke, 'Gregorian Reform in Action', in his *Medieval Church and Society,* 1972, 94.

personnel by lay lords. The leaders of the church should be elected by the clergy or monks who would be committed to their charge, and the election should be scrutinised by higher ecclesiastical authority. In this selection process the king should have no part. This represented a doctrine of revolution; it was an assault on the custom of centuries. Yet, as Gregory VII sharply remarked, 'The Lord hath not said "I am custom", but He hath said "I am the truth"'.[5] The papal circle honestly believed that in demanding the liberty of the church they were fulfilling God's plan for justice on earth. Naturally their plans met with the fiercest resistance from those whose customary rights were threatened, and the Investiture Contest was marked by prolonged intellectual and physical violence in Italy and Germany.[6] In the face of opposition the reformers' demands became ever more extreme. Their insistence on the freedom of the church was developed into an assertion that for the right order of society it was necessary that even kings should be subject to the clerical hierarchy, culminating in the pope, since only the priesthood was qualified to interpret God's ordinance.

In the late eleventh century, therefore, two philosophies of world government came into conflict - the old order of an integrated church and society under the aegis of a sacerdotal king, ruling as God's deputy on earth, the

---

5 H.E.J. Cowdrey, ed., *The* Epistolae Vagantes *of Pope Gregory VII*, Oxford 1972, Appx. A no. 67.

6 For a convenient selection of key letters, see B. Tierney, *The Crisis of Church and State, 1050-1300,* Englewood Cliffs 1964, 45-73; for extensive analysis, I.S. Robinson, *Authority and Resistance in the Investiture Contest,* Manchester 1978.

world as it had been under the Emperor Constantine in the fourth century, under Charlemagne in the eighth and under the successors of Alfred in tenth-century England; and the projected new order of a united Christian commonwealth under the ultimate authority of the successor of St. Peter at Rome. The history of the church in England in the century after the Conquest is, in one important sense, the development of a compromise between these two ideological systems, based on the realities of power and thus normally favouring the king, who was on the spot and who possessed the means of coercion by physical intimidation and persuasion by the exercise of his extensive patronage. The king, however, could never entirely ignore the new ideas emanating from Rome, and in moments of weakness, such as the uncertain successions of 1100 and 1135, the balance could tip the other way.

The Late Old-English Church

The tenth century had been an heroic period in the history of the English church.[7] Religious life had been reconstructed after the devastation caused by the Viking invasions. This renewal had been accomplished by an alliance between the kings of Wessex and a group of outstanding monastic bishops who sought the regeneration of society by the application of principles expressed in the Rule of St. Benedict. This alliance achieved its

---

7 C.J. Godfrey, *The Church in Anglo-Saxon England,* Cambridge 1962, 294-309; M. Deanesly, *The Pre-Conquest Church in England,* 1961, 276-327.

greatest triumphs in the reign of King Edgar (959-78), during which freedom from external attack was utilised as an opportunity both to consolidate the royal hold over an expanding realm and to reassert the moral influence of the Christian church. Whereas on the continent those intent on religious reform believed that this could best be achieved by the emancipation of the church from secular control (a programme symbolised by the foundation of Cluny in 911 as a monastery immune from all authority save that of St. Peter), in England the strength of a king 'by God's authority, confirmed through the bishops and other servants of God'[8] was seen as the best guarantee of the spiritual welfare of the kingdom.

A century later William of Normandy advanced the degeneracy of the English church as a further justification for the invasion to secure his rights. Writing two generations after the Conquest the historian William of Malmesbury, himself of mixed parentage and deeply respectful of Anglo-Saxon Christian tradition, believed that religion had become totally moribund during the last years of the Old English kingdom and was revived by the Normans.[9] Was the decline as marked as the Conqueror's propaganda and the chronicler's judgement would suggest?

Much hinges on the view which is taken of Stigand,

---

8 For Edgar's coronation and its significance, see P.H. Sawyer, *From Roman Britain to Norman England*, 1978, 184-8.

9 D.C. Douglas and G.W. Greenway, *English Historical Documents* ii, *1042-1189*, 1968, 290-1.

archbishop of Canterbury, who had been intruded into the primatial see, by the influence of the Godwin family, after the expulsion in 1052 of the Norman archbishop Robert of Jumièges, and who never resigned his former bishopric of Winchester.[10] Stigand's anomalous position is, in fact, a reflection of the way in which the leadership of the church had become enmeshed in the factional conflicts which characterised the last phase of the Old English state. Edward the Confessor himself, in the years of his greatest independence, had preferred household clerks to holy monks when filling bishoprics, and prelates other than Stigand were pluralists; Leofric abbot of Peterborough, for example, obtained the rule of four other monasteries. Even in the most blatant cases of irregularity, however, there is need for some qualification. Stigand himself was noted for his generosity to religious houses, despite the fact that his uncanonical position led English bishops to go to the continent for consecration. His colleague in the north, Ealdred, was noted as an advocate of reform who 'raised the see of York from its former rustic state'.[11] Leofgar bishop of Hereford was regarded with some suspicion because of his military enthusiasm, yet it should be remembered that in 1098 the papal legate personally commanded a division of the crusading army before Antioch.

To a great extent, the 'decline' was due to the failure of

---

10 For a recent, unfavourable, assessment, see N. Brooks, *The Early History of the Church of Canterbury*, Leicester 1984, 304-10.

11 For Ealdred, see J. Cooper, *The Last Four Anglo-Saxon Archbishops of York*, Borthwick Papers 38, York 1970, 23-9.

8

the English church, 'on the outer edge of the earth's extent',[12] to keep pace with the remarkable transformation of the Roman see. During the long eclipse of papal authority from the ninth to the early eleventh centuries, it had been English initiative which had maintained contact, by the payment of Peter's Pence (annual tribute originally levied from every household) and through the visits of archbishops to the apostolic see to receive their pallium, the symbol of their office. In 1046 papal permission was sought for the move of the bishopric of Crediton to Exeter, a transfer which foreshadowed the modernising site-changes accomplished after the Conquest. Despite the self-conscious loyalty of the English church to Rome, however, the reforming council held by Leo IX at Rheims in 1049 seems to have made more impact in Normandy than in the island kingdom, although nothing in fact was promulgated there that had not been foreshadowed in English royal legislation of the tenth and early eleventh centuries. It is perhaps significant that the foremost surviving advocates of reform in England, Wulfstan bishop of Worcester and Aethelwig abbot of Evesham, chose after 1066 to work in association with the Normans, even acting as William's local governmental agents, in much the same way as progressive Irish bishops after 1171 placed their trust in Henry II.[13] Yet if the spirit of reform generally was petering out in England just at the time when it was gathering force at Rome, and was eventually mediated through Rouen and Bec, it would be unjust to judge the

---

12 For England as 'another world', see R.W. Southern, *Medieval Humanism and Other Studies*, Oxford 1970, 133.
13 J.A. Watt, *The Church and the Two Nations in Medieval Ireland*, Cambridge 1970, 39.

state of the English church in the 1050s by the highest standards of the Gregorian papacy.

That the English church was not moribund is perhaps best illustrated by the strenuous efforts of missionaries from the island kingdom to evangelise Scandinavia.[14] Their campaign spans the Norman Conquest, beginning around 995 with those English priests who assisted King Olaf Trygvason in his forcible conversion of Norway. Sigfrid, a monk of Glastonbury, was the first missionary bishop in Sweden; another Englishman, Tursgot, around 1020 became the first Swedish diocesan bishop, and their work was continued by David, who died around 1080 and was subsequently canonised. During the reign of Cnut the Great, ruler of a double kingdom, English missionaries began to appear in Denmark and after the Conquest, in Rufus's reign, the great Danish monastery of Odense was founded from Evesham in Worcestershire.[15] The impetus continued well into the twelfth century, and in the 1150s the English St. Henry of Finland initiated the conversion of the most remote area of Scandinavia. The total achievement falls not far short of that of St. Boniface of Crediton in the eighth century.

The Norman Model

The contrast between the Norman and English churches

---

14 C.J.A. Oppermann, *The English Missionaries in Sweden and Finland*, 1937.

15 P. King, 'English Influence on the Church at Odense in the Early Middle Ages', *Journal of Ecclesiastical History* 13, 1962, 145-55.

in the quarter century before the Conquest can be explained in large measure by the consideration that the church in the duchy was undergoing then much the same experience as had that of the kingdom in Edgar's reign.[16] The need for the reconstruction of religion in Normandy had been even more urgent than in England, for the new rulers in the tenth century had been the erstwhile pagan Vikings. Yet by the 1060s the Normans were noted throughout Christendom for their particularly militant brand of Christianity. For the duke and his greater vassals, the acceptance of the faith guaranteed their reception into the aristocratic community of Western Europe. The people followed their lead, encouraged no doubt by many incidents, such as those described by Bede in seventh-century England, when the magic of the Christian God proved more potent than that of the ancient Scandinavian pantheon. The transformation is easier to understand if it is remembered that the Christian religion did not become Christocentric until the twelfth century at the earliest; God was still very much the Old Testament tribal deity who favoured His chosen people and aided them in battle. Norman religion has been well described as 'a theology of armed action',[17] which was given practical expression as much in the conquest of England as in Southern Italy, Sicily, Spain and a few years later on the First Crusade.

As in tenth-century England, the reconstruction of Christianity in eleventh-century Normandy was the achieve-

---

16 For a survey of the church in pre-Conquest Normandy, see D. Bates, *Normandy before 1066*, 1982, 189-235.

17 D.C. Douglas, *The Norman Achievement*, 1969, 101.

ment of the ruling dynasty in alliance with zealous Benedictine missionaries. The monastic expansion, which
resulted in the establishment between 1000 and 1070 of
thirty-three religious houses, was assiduously furthered
by the dukes as a means of fostering political unity, but
by mid-century the secular aristocracy were also enthusiastic patrons of the monks. The second stage of Chris-
tianisation was marked by the re-establishment of defined dioceses, and over his bishops the duke also maintained firm control. William's agents on the episcopal
bench were men of diverse character. Archbishop Mau-
rilius at Rouen (1054-67) held the first effective reforming councils and issued the initial prohibition in the duchy
of clerical marriage. Odo of Bayeux (*c.* 1049-97), half-
brother of the duke, was immune to the moral strictures
of the reformers and was intent on secular aggrandize-
ment; he was, nevertheless, the creator of a well-organ-
ised diocese and of a cathedral chapter noted for its
intellectual attainment.[18] By 1080 Duke William, through
a mixture of conventional piety and political shrewd-
ness, had created an episcopate noted for 'a professional
quality which was outstanding in contemporary northern
France'.[19] Clear contrary to the ideology of the Roman
reformers, he presided in person over synods of the province of Rouen in which bishops and abbots met to prom-
ulgate measures which fostered both the observance of
the faith and the consolidation of ducal authority. Most
significantly, in 1047 the Truce of God was proclaimed
in an attempt to curb internal violence which threatened

---

18 D. Bates, 'The Character and Career of Odo, Bishop of Bayeux
(1049/50-97)', *Speculum* 50, 1975, 1-20.

19 Bates, *Normandy before 1066*, 212.

both the peace of the church and the security of the duchy. It is noteworthy that lay investiture was never discussed at these meetings, and that at the Council of Lillebonne in 1080 it was decreed that if secular and ecclesiastical jurisdictions should clash, arbitration between them pertained to the duke.[20]

A recent historian of the duchy has passed a severe judgement on William's ecclesiastical policy. His control of the church was 'a carefully calculated operation' and his attitudes 'those of a proprietor, not a benefactor'.[21] This verdict is, perhaps, excessively harsh. If the Conqueror was prone initially to pillage churches associated with his enemies, both in north-western France and in England, contrition and piety combined to make him one of the great monastic patrons of an age noted for lavish benefaction. The papacy recognised him as an outstanding Christian prince and a champion of reform, albeit one not prepared to accept the most radical assertions of Roman supremacy over a united western Christendom. The Norman church was aggressively orthodox; duke and bishops accepted without question the doctrinal authority of the apostolic see and the desirability of those moral reforms which it advocated. Their implementation was attempted, however, within a self-contained ecclesiastical province in which papal legates intervened only at ducal invitation and outside which Norman prelates seldom ventured.

---

20 R. Foreville, 'The Synod of the Province of Rouen in the Eleventh and Twelfth Centuries', in C.N.L. Brooke *et al.*, eds. *Church and Government in the Middle Ages*, Cambridge 1976, 19-40.

21 Bates, *Normandy before 1066*, 206-7.

The same model of reform was to be applied in England after 1066. It must be emphasised, however, that reforming activity in the duchy reached its peak only in the 1060s and 1070s, and much remained to be done at home after the conquest of England. Orderic Vitalis commented on those priests of Danish extraction who, when confronted by the demand that they should abandon both their concubines and the pursuit of arms, were more ready to renounce their weapons than their women. In 1072 the bishop of Avranches was stoned by the priests of his diocese when he urged on them in synod the need for celibacy.[22] Equally significant, the plantation of Benedictine monasticism as an agency of reform and a vehicle of ducal authority was occurring in western Normandy at exactly the same time as in the north of England. Both areas had hitherto been immune to modern trends in religion and to centralised secular control; they felt simultaneously the impact of a reform movement which was papally inspired but monarchically directed.

Domination and Accommodation

All over England, although particularly in outlying and border areas, the Normans used the church as an agent of colonisation. By the end of the Conqueror's reign the episcopate had been almost totally Normanised, most of the wealthy churches throughout the island had passed into the hands of influential clerics from north-western

---

22 M. Chibnall, ed., *The Ecclesiastical History of Orderic Vitalis*, Oxford 1969-80, iii, 121-3; ii, 201.

France, and the greater abbeys too were ruled by members of the conquering race.[23] The religious houses of the duchy received their share of the spoils by the grant of English estates - the place-name Tooting Bec, now in South London, is testimony to one such gift.[24] The foundation by William of Battle abbey on the site of his great victory is one symbol of the role of the church in the Conquest - a privileged royal church which served as a war-memorial;[25] as also, to take one example of many, are the Sussex town of Lewes and the Norfolk village of Acre, in both of which William de Warenne built great castles and planted colonies of French monks from the Burgundian abbey of Cluny.[26] The harrying of the North in 1069-70 was followed up by the foundation of numerous monasteries (of which there had been none north of Ely in 1066) as well as by construction of motte and bailey fortifications. The new style of Romanesque architecture, ecclesiastical building on a scale never before seen in England, was itself a visual symbol of the new lordship, and if the historian concentrates on the great masterpieces at Durham, Winchester and St. Albans, it

23 D.S. Spear, 'The Norman Empire and the Secular Clergy, 1066-1204', *Journal of British Studies* 21, 1982, 1-10.

24 D. Matthew, *The Norman Monasteries and their English Possessions*, Oxford 1962, 26-71; M. Morgan, *The English Lands of the Abbey of Bec*, Oxford 1946, part 1.

25 E.M. Hallam, 'Monasteries as "War Memorials": Battle Abbey and La Victoire', *Studies in Church History* 20, 1983, 47-57.

26 B. Golding, 'The Coming of the Cluniacs', *Anglo-Norman Studies* 3, 1981, 65-77, (notes) 208-10.

should be remembered that the new dispensation was marked by the rebuilding of almost every parish and conventual church in England.[27]

Domination and ostentation were not, however, the only features of the Anglo-Norman church. At an early date there were clear signs of accommodation with the Old English past. There were, of course, isolated scandalous incidents, most famously the intimidation by the new abbot of Glastonbury of his native monastic congregation; but the culprit was removed from office by Lanfranc.[28] The archbishop himself was certainly dubious about the merits of undocumented Anglo-Saxon saints, whose veneration he regarded as a distraction from true religion, but once a case for sanctity was properly demonstrated, as in the case of St. Alphege of Canterbury, he accepted and encouraged observance of the feast. The cults of Cuthbert at Durham, Edmund in his Suffolk borough and Etheldreda at Ely were eagerly taken up by the Normans; these saints were venerated for religious reasons, but also utilised for political purposes.[29] The great eighth-century historian Bede was a source of inspiration to Norman monks, historians and founders, while the abandoned site of St. Hilda's abbey at Whitby prompted

---

27 For a general survey of the Norman architectural impact, see T. Rowley, *The Norman Heritage, 1066-1200*, 1983, chapter 4.

28 M.D. Knowles, *The Monastic Order in England*, Cambridge 1940, 114-5.

29 S.J. Ridyard, '*Condigna Veneratio*: Post-Conquest Attitudes to the Saints of the Anglo-Saxons', *Anglo-Norman Studies* 9, 1987, 179-206.

the conversion to religion of the knight Reinfrid, engaged on the devastation of the north, to which he returned with English monks from Evesham as a Benedictine pioneer.[30] In the early twelfth century Anglo-Saxon and Anglo-Scandinavian hermits such as Godric of Finchale, Wulfric of Haselbury and Christina of Markyate acted as intercessors and mediators between native populace and priests and their new ecclesiastical masters, but they were eagerly accepted by Norman religious communities as holy assets and spiritual capital.[31] The Norman aristocracy, too, soon came to terms with their new environment and abandoned their cross-Channel spiritual yearnings. Within a generation, the majority were choosing English rather than Norman burial-places, and there are instances of gifts to monasteries in the duchy being transferred to insular houses.[32] Conversely, surviving English landholders became benefactors of French foundations; an obscure native merchant, Ailwin Child, was the true founder of the Cluniac house at Bermondsey in 1089, and older Cumbrian families contributed to the endowments of monasteries founded by Anglo-Nor-

---

30 R.H.C. Davies, 'Bede after Bede', in C. Harper-Bill, C. Holdsworth and J.L. Nelson, eds., *Studies in Medieval History presented to R. Allen Brown*, Woodbridge 1989, 103-16.

31 H. Mayr-Harting, 'Functions of a Twelfth-Century Recluse', *History* 60, 1975, 337-52.

32 B. Golding, 'Anglo-Norman Knightly Burials', in C. Harper-Bill and R. Harvey, eds., *The Ideals and Practice of Medieval Knighthood* i, Woodbridge 1986, 35-48; E. Mason, 'English Tithe Income of Norman Religious Houses', *Bulletin of Institute of Historical Research* 48, 1975, 91-4.

man lords in the north-west.[33] The confraternity list of Rochester cathedral priory contains a healthy mixture of English and French names, united in their devotion and benefactions to St. Andrew.[34]

The effect of the Conquest on the wealth of the English church is not a clear-cut matter.[35] Much of its landed endowment had been lost during the Viking invasions, and far from all the losses had been recovered during the tenth-century reformation, even before Scandinavian pressure resumed during Ethelred's reign. English monastic chronicles complained bitterly of Norman depredation, yet on occasion the diminution of a church's estates can be demonstrated to have pre-dated 1066. Christ Church Canterbury, for example, had suffered more from the misappropriations of Earl Godwin than of Odo of Bayeux, who was accused by Archbishop Lanfranc of detaching its lands. Domesday Book shows ecclesiastical losses to Norman lords to have been insubstantial, usually of outlying manors. The church did, however, suffer through the Conqueror's imposition of knight service upon the bishoprics and greater abbeys. The

---

33 D. Knowles and R.N. Hadcock, *Medieval Religious Houses, England and Wales*, 2nd edn 1971, 98; R.K. Rose, 'Cumbrian Society and the Anglo-Norman Church', *Studies in Church History* 18, 1982, 119-35.

34 H. Tsurushima, 'The Fraternity of Rochester Cathedral Priory about 1100', *Anglo-Norman Studies* 14 (forthcoming).

35 The following paragraph is based on A. Ayton and V. Davis, 'Ecclesiastical Wealth in England in 1086', *Studies in Church History* 24, 1987, 47-60.

land of England was listed at around £73,000 in 1086; of this, £18,400 was held by the ecclesiastical tenants-in-chief, but £3,500 of this was subinfeudated to provide for military obligations (and many knights, too, were still maintained in the households of bishops and abbots). Out of about 5000 knights owed, 741½ were due from the church. Yet despite this substantial burden, there can be little doubt that ecclesiastical wealth did increase, except perhaps in the south of the country where the church had been so well endowed before the Conquest. In Lincolnshire, for example, the church's proportion of landed resources increased between 1065 and 1086 from 2% to 12%. Domesday Book, moreover, was produced a generation too early to reflect the real impact of the Conquest, for at least twenty-six Benedictine communities and six Cluniac houses were founded between 1086 and 1100, and thereafter Norman lords were extremely generous patrons of the new Augustinian and Cistercian orders. Domesday Book, moreover, hardly reflects the Norman ecclesiastical impact on the North.

In terms of organisation, the Conquest brought obvious changes to the English church. The institutions of the Old English church had been old-fashioned, and continental bishops were eager to modernise - although there was no need for the creation of territorial dioceses or the elimination of hereditary abbacies, as there would be when the reform movement permeated into Wales and Ireland. English sees were moved from rural sites to thriving centres of population - among others, Dorchester was transferred to Lincoln, Selsey to Chichester, Sherborne to Old Sarum (later Salisbury).[36] Within the secular cathedrals there was established the continental model of chapter, in which the responsibility for liturgy, education and financial administration was allocated to three major officers serving under the presidency of a dean, and in which the church's revenues were in large part divided between the prebendaries, senior and distinguished clerks, many of whom would be non-resident.[37] This was a retrograde step from Old English attempts to establish a communal life for cathedral clergy, but reflected the need of king and bishops to provide lucrative livings for valued administrators. Despite such practical considerations, however, the Normans greatly approved of the Anglo-Saxon monastic cathedrals, an institution unknown elsewhere in western Europe, and established new ones at Durham, Norwich and elsewhere.

Of more immediate significance to the great majority of English people was the reorganisation of the church's jurisdictional structure. The Anglo-Saxon bishop had sat as joint-president of the shire court, alongside earl or sheriff; there he administered royal law which, under the influence of the tenth-century monastic reformers, legislated as much against sin as against crime. Between 1072 and 1085 the Conqueror issued an ordinance which has traditionally been interpreted as separating lay and ecclesiastical jurisdiction and establishing independent

36 For one case, see D.M. Owen, 'The Norman Cathedral at Lincoln', *Anglo-Norman Studies* 6, 1983, 188-99.

37 D. Greenway, 'Orders and Rank in the Cathedral of Old Sarum', *Studies in Church History* 26, 1989, 55-63.

church courts - a dichotomy which was to cause much dissention a century later. It has been convincingly argued, however, that the intention was not to remove the bishop from the shire court, but rather to allow him to hold his own courts as well, so that jurisdiction, and its profits, should now pertain in moral matters exclusively to the church.[38] Episcopal justice was henceforth exercised most publicly in synods, regular meetings of the clergy of the diocese, which served also to communicate to grass-roots level the legislation of provincial, and even papal, councils. There is evidence for a synod convened by Wulfstan of Worcester in 1092, and by the early twelfth century such were held in most, if not all, dioceses. Even more important, the archdeacon, newly introduced to England after 1066 as the bishop's judicial officer, should be able to hold his own courts, so that spiritual cases would no longer be decided in the local hundred courts, presided over by the sheriff. It was the establishment of a network of local ecclesiastical courts, held at regular meetings of the clergy of each rural deanery (a grouping of about twenty churches) under the presidency of the archdeacon, which allowed the application in the parishes of the new canon law introduced from the continent by Archbishop Lanfranc, a code which was rapidly evolving in the late eleventh and early twelfth centuries and which was increasingly Roman and universal rather than regional and dependent for enforcement on royal officers, as had been the case in Anglo-

---

38 C. Morris, 'William I and the Church Courts', *English Historical Review* 82, 1967, 449-63; D.J.A. Matthew, *The Norman Conquest*, 1966, 193-5.

Scandinavian England.[39] The effectiveness of the arch-
deacons' courts in enforcing new norms of sexual morality and religious observance, most often by financial
penalties, is indicated by the reputation for greed and
extortion which these officials had already achieved by
the mid-twelfth century.

The Investiture Contest in England

The relationship between the papacy, the crown and the
English church was complex.[40] In general terms there
was quite remarkable cordiality between William the
Conqueror and Rome.[41] In one sense the king was a
disappointment to the pope, for in 1080 he conclusively
rejected Gregory VII's demand that England should be
held as a fief of the apostolic see, in the same way that
the Norman duchies of southern Italy were theoretically
dependent upon Rome. Yet despite this rejection Gregory recognised that William was a supporter of the
programme of moral reform advocated by the papacy.
In comparison with Henry IV of Germany he was a loyal

---

39 J. Scammel, 'The Rural Chapter in England from the Eleventh to
the Fourteenth Centuries', *English Historical Review* 86, 1971, 1-
21.

40 For general survey, see C. Duggan, 'From the Conquest to the
Reign of John', in C.H. Lawrence, ed., *The English Church and the
Papacy in the Middle Ages*, 1965, 63-116.

41 H.E.J. Cowdrey, 'Pope Gregory VII and the Anglo-Norman Church
and Kingdom', in his *Popes, Monks and Crusaders*, 1984, chapter
9.

son of the church, alongside Philip I of France he was a model of Christian morality. The Conqueror, confronted throughout his reign by challengers for his throne, and the pope, continually faced by imperial aggression, needed each other. The position of Archbishop Lanfranc was ambiguous. He came to Canterbury in 1070 as the favourite son of the papacy, the triumphant defender of doctrinal orthodoxy. Relations were soured by the failure of Rome to give whole-hearted support to Canterbury's claim for primacy over all the churches of the British Isles, which was achieved, in the key matter of the relationship between the two English archbishoprics, and albeit ambiguously and temporarily, by the decision of a royal council rather than by papal decree. Lanfranc was an enthusiastic advocate of the reform programme initiated by Leo IX; by the 1080s he appears to have been cautious in the extreme in his support for Gregory VII's world-view.

Lanfranc's successor, Anselm, faced a very different situation.[42] He was appointed by William Rufus in 1093, after a long vacancy at Canterbury, only because the king thought himself at death's door. The new archbishop then insisted on recognising Urban II, rather than the rival imperial pope, before the king had announced his own decision. The king's attempt to rid himself of this aged and troublesome archbishop in return for royal

---

42 For Anselm, see R.W. Southern, *St Anselm and his Biographer*, Cambridge 1963, and his latest treatment in *St Anselm: a Portrait in a Landscape*, Cambridge 1990; also S.N. Vaughn, *Anselm of Bec and Robert of Meulan: the Innocence of the Dove and the Wisdom of the Serpent*, Berkeley 1987.

recognition of Urban (which was a political necessity) misfired when the papal legate refused to keep his side of the bargain by deposing Anselm. The relationship between England and Rome therefore came, largely through Rufus's misjudgment, to centre stage, and this dispute, only superficially resolved, was the backdrop to the quarrel between king and archbishop in 1097 over the allegedly unsatisfactory discharge of the military obligations of the see of Canterbury. The altercation over the quality of the Canterbury knights led to Anselm's first exile, and it was his sojourn at the papal court, and his presence at the councils of Bari and Rome in 1098-99, where he heard Urban II condemn both lay investiture and the rendering of homage to laymen for the lands of the church, which brought the investiture controversy to England.

The new king, Henry I, despite his desire for reconciliation with the archbishop, could not afford to abandon homage for the extensive lands held by the church in England. Anselm now felt, as he had not before, bound to refuse that homage for the Canterbury estates, and so went into exile again in 1103. Eventually, when Henry was desperate for papal sanction of his conquest of Normandy from his eldest brother, a compromise was reached in 1106 at the abbey of Bec, which was ratified next year by the Council of Westminster. The king abandoned investiture with ring and staff, thus ceasing to intrude on the conferment of *spiritual* office, but was permitted to take the homage of bishops- and abbots-elect for their *temporalities* before their consecration. This, in effect, gave the crown the power of veto, for ecclesiastical estates, accumulated over centuries and now burdened with military obligations, were in reality inseparable from any major church. This compromise ended the so-called 'investiture contest' in England, to which kingdom it had been late in coming, and it provided a model for the settlement in 1122 of the far more bitter struggle in the Empire. Pope Paschal II wrote to Anselm expressing the hope that the king would make further concessions, specifically the renunciation of homage, but in essentials the arrangements agreed in 1106 remained in force until the Reformation. Elections, it was agreed, should be free, but they were normally held in the royal chapel, with the cathedral chapter represented by a small delegation which could easily be persuaded, or intimidated, by the king. In terms of personnel, which was the key issue, the compromise changed little. Rufus had appointed Ranulf Flambard, his financial agent, and Robert Bloet, his chancellor, to bishoprics; after 1106 Henry I nominated his trusted servant William Warelwast to Exeter and his nephew Henry of Blois to Winchester.

Lanfranc and Anselm

The contrast between the cooperation which was the norm between 1070 and 1088 and the intermittent conflict which prevailed from 1093 to 1107 has often been viewed as a measure of the different characters and attitudes of Lanfranc and Anselm. The first post-Conquest archbishop of Canterbury acted in concert with William I to introduce moral reform of the church, yet sought to preserve the independence from Rome of an integrated Anglo-Norman church under the firm control of the king-duke. His successor not only had a more thorough approach to the reform of the clergy, seeking to abolish clerical marriage instantly rather than allowing it to wither away; he also endeavoured to protect the independence of the English church from the secular ruler, rather than from the pope, in his obedience to whom he was unswerving. It has recently been suggested, however, that there was in fact a strong element of continuity in the programmes of the two archbishops.[43]

Lanfranc's reputation has been rather strangely diminished in modern accounts.[44] He has been viewed as a derivative theologian and, as archbishop, passively acquiescent towards the king's wishes. The most recent treatment of his career before 1063, however, seeks to restore his reputation as 'a major force in the political and intellectual life of his times', who was instrumental in establishing the Catholic doctrine of transubstantiation, whose views radiated outwards from his school at Bec which was the foremost educational institution of the age, and who did much to mould Duke William's attitudes towards reform.[45] For most of Lanfranc's archiepiscopate western Europe was racked by the most bitter phase of the investiture controversy. If in retrospect

---

43 C. Warren Hollister, 'St Anselm on Lay Investiture', *Anglo-Norman Studies* 10, 1988, 145-58.

44 M. Gibson, *Lanfranc of Bec*, Oxford 1978; F. Barlow, 'A View of Archbishop Lanfranc', *Journal of Ecclesiastical History* 16, 1965, 163-77, reprinted in his *The Norman Conquest and Beyond*, 1983, 223-38.

45 S.N. Vaughn, 'Lanfranc at Bec: a Reinterpretation', *Albion* 17, 1985, 135-48.

Gregory VII may be seen as the architect of the medieval papacy, during his lifetime his policies tore the church
apart; from June 1080 there was genuine doubt as to
whether he or the imperial 'anti-pope' Clement III was
the rightful pontiff, and he died in exile deserted by
most of his own cardinals. Lanfranc's ambiguous attitude to such a pope, who moreover had done nothing to
support the primatial claims which were the birthright of
the church of Canterbury, does not indicate mere subser-
vience to the Conqueror. The archbishop as much as the
king was unwilling that the governance of the Anglo-
Norman church should be undermined by the intrusion
of papal legates despatched from Rome, whose authority
would override his own. He accepted without reserva-
tion the doctrinal supremacy of Rome, while eschewing
aims which he felt impossible, such as the immediate
deprivation of priests already, and in accordance with
age-old custom, married. He did not feel bound to approach Rome for approval in all those jurisdictional or
administrative matters in which the papacy increasingly
claimed omnicompetence - the transfer of numerous sees,
for example, was accomplished without reference to the
curia. Lanfranc avoided conflict with a king who was
himself an advocate of reform; he supervised the organisational changes which shaped the structure of the English church until the Reformation;[46] and despite the primacy dispute and isolated conflicts with individual bishops, he was able to hold together an episcopal bench

---

46 'It may be doubted whether of all the eminent men who filled
the see of Canterbury between Augustine and Cranmer any individual,
save only Theodore of Tarsus, had a greater share in organising the
church in this country.' Knowles, *Monastic Order*, 143.

containing a mixture of Benedictine monks, royal clerks and Norman aristocrats, and to postpone the impact of the investiture controversy on England. It was no small achievement.

Anselm has often been viewed as a 'papalist' archbishop, bound by his monastic vow of obedience to follow unswervingly the dictates of Rome, and thus unable to tolerate that working arrangement with the king which Lanfranc regarded as the surest guarantee of gradual reform; twice he preferred exile to accommodation. There were, however, important differences in the conditions under which the two archbishops operated. The reputation of William Rufus has been considerably enhanced by recent studies,[47] yet there can be no doubt that he did ruthlessly exploit the church during the vacancy of bishoprics and abbeys and that the holding of reforming councils was suspended during his reign. The Conqueror, however tight his control over the church, had not resorted to such abuse or obstruction, which it is extremely unlikely that Lanfranc could have tolerated. There was, too, a substantial difference in the condition of the papacy. By the time of Anselm's first exile in 1097, Urban II had begun the reestablishment of the 'Gregorian line' of popes as the natural leaders of the western church, maintaining a firm line on reforming policies yet uniting the aristocracy of northern Europe by the launching of the First Crusade and seeking accommodation with former enemies within the ranks of the higher clergy. By 1099 'he had really made himself

---

47 F. Barlow, *William Rufus*, 1983; E. Mason, 'William Rufus and the Historians', *Medieval History* I i, 1991, 6-22.

the head of the greater part of Christendom',[48] and after
September 1100 there was no serious anti-pope to challenge his successor, Paschal II.

Anselm was, no more than Lanfranc, an uncompromising Gregorian. He was as adamant as his predecessor in
his defence of Canterbury's primacy, which ran counter
to papal policy favouring co-equal archbishoprics directly
dependent on Rome, and he was firmly opposed to the
entry into England of legates despatched directly by the
pope. It is impossible that he should not have heard of
earlier papal condemnations of lay investiture and the
rendering of homage, especially that pronounced by Urban II at Clermont in 1095, yet he did not raise these
issues in England. After he had personally heard the
pope's decrees in 1098-99, however, he could not keep
silent. By this time, moreover, he had first-hand experience of the aggressive nature of Rufus's ecclesiastical
policy. It is instructive that, despite Anselm's stand, the
investiture controversy never attained in England the same
level of intensity as it did in Germany and northern
Italy. It might have been avoided altogether, as it was in
France, if Anselm had not been driven into his first exile
by Rufus's intransigence.

Over Anselm's motivation in his relationship with the
English crown there has recently been some disagree-
ment between Sir Richard Southern and Professor Sally
Vaughn.[49] It is perfectly possible to believe, with South-

---

48 C. Morris, *The Papal Monarchy: the Western Church from 1050
to 1250*, Oxford 1989, 126.

49 See note 42, and more specifically R.W. Southern, 'Sally Vaughn's

ern, that Anselm did not desire the archbishopric, that his resistance to his appointment was no charade but rather 'the cry of an anguished soul who sees himself threatened with separation from his long and intense struggle towards the knowledge of God', to reject utterly Vaughn's suggestion that he lingered deliberately in England in 1092-93 in the hope that Rufus would eventually advance him to Canterbury, and yet to consider that he was prepared to accept God's will when it was made manifest, to undertake a burden from which he had earnestly sought release, and thereafter to fulfil the obligations of his stewardship in every possible way. The Benedictine ideal most certainly lay at the heart of Anselm's endeavours in every field, but the monastic tradition did not encourage, for prelates at least, introspective withdrawal from the affairs of the world. Once he had unwillingly accepted the archbishopric, Anselm was obliged to capitalise on the friendship network which he had established with great and powerful men in the Anglo-Norman realm - and he had a remarkable gift for disinterested affection - to foster the welfare of the church in general and the see of Canterbury in particular. There was nothing dishonourable in this; indeed, to have failed to capitalise on his connections would have been a denial of his responsibilities to God and to the church. Vaughn's view of 'the philosopher-saint as politician' is unfortunate,[50] since the concept of ecclesiastical politics in the late eleventh century is anachronistic. Anselm,

Anselm: an Examination of the Foundations' and S.N. Vaughn, 'Anselm: Saint and Statesman', *Albion* 20, 1988, 181-220.

50 S.N. Vaughn, 'St Anselm of Canterbury: the Philosopher-Saint as Politician', *Journal of Medieval History* 1, 1975, 279-305.

like all his contemporaries in religion, surely regarded
the 'management' of his lay friends as a worthy activity
if designed, as it always was, to further the advancement
of God's kingdom on earth, the ultimate aim of all the
reforming circle. Anselm sought the well-being (*utilitas*) of the church of Bec, the church of Canterbury and
the church universal, and by this he meant spiritual well-being. Yet he was realistic enough to know that the
church must exist in the world - his writings are permeated by the feudal images of his contemporary environment. As abbot he desired to extend the benefits of the
monastic life to the countryside around Bec; so as archbishop he saw the Rule of St. Benedict as an ideal for
society as a whole. In this he was little different from
St. Dunstan in the tenth century or from his immediate
predecessor, Lanfranc. He was certainly not like his
contemporaries Henry I and Count Robert of Meulan, or
even his own episcopal colleagues, in his vision of the
church, for he was undoubtedly a spiritual genius; but
neither was he incapable of entering into their world in
the hope and expectation of transforming it to correspond more nearly to the divine model.

The Predominance of Local Interests

Anselm's archiepiscopate witnessed the first episode in
England of what is conventionally known as a 'crisis of
church and state', which is one of the predominant themes
of western European history between the late eleventh
and early fourteenth centuries. Yet how meaningful is
this concept? In speaking of a conflict between *regnum*
and *sacerdotium* there must at least be many qualifica-

tions. The bishopric and the abbatial office had a dual nature, which the ardent reformers repudiated but which all practical men recognised. The bishop was not only father in God to those souls committed to his charge and judge of their moral behaviour; he was also a baron, a tenant-in-chief of the crown. He was responsible for the management of extensive estates; the value of the lordship of Canterbury was exceeded only by that of the royal demesne,[51] and the richer bishoprics were as valuable as any lay barony. Military service was owed on a scale commensurate with this wealth. The bishop of Lincoln was likely more at home in his castle at Sleaford than in his cathedral, the abbot of Bury St. Edmunds was constantly occupied with the king's government in West Suffolk.[52] The saintly bishop Gundulf of Rochester appears in his biography as the type of the ideal monk and pastor, yet he was also the military architect who supervised the building of the Tower of London.[53] Even Anselm, despite his dispute with Rufus over the Canterbury knights, regarded it as his duty to superintend the defence of the south coast while the king campaigned in the north, where guarding the frontier was one of the paramount duties of the bishop of Durham.

---

51 M. Brett, *The English Church under Henry I*, Oxford 1975, 69.

52 For example, see A. Gransden, 'Baldwin, Abbot of Bury St Edmunds', *Anglo-Norman Studies* 4, 1982, 65-76.

53 For Gundulf, see R.A.L. Smith, 'The Place of Gundulf in the Anglo-Norman Church', *English Historical Review* 58, 1943, 257-72, reprinted in his *Collected Papers*, 1947, 83-102; M. Ruud, 'Monks in the World: the Case of Gundulf of Rochester', *Anglo-Norman Studies* 11, 1989, 245-60.

When the conflict between Anselm and Rufus broke into
the open in 1095 at the Council of Rockingham, the
bishops almost to a man supported the king. The archbishop's backing came from the lay barons, resentful of
the new and grasping style of kingship which threatened
secular as well as ecclesiastical estates. This indicates
the gross simplification in speaking of a conflict of church
and state, but on reflection it is hardly surprising. Of
Anselm's thirteen episcopal colleagues at the time he
first went into exile, eight had been royal chaplains whose
services, not only by prayer, had been rewarded with a
bishopric; three of these men had been chancellor. They
had been the executors, in some cases perhaps the for-
mulators, of royal policy, and it would have been unreal-
istic to expect that they would suddenly abandon the
habits of a lifetime, risk the loss of royal favour and
patronage and endanger the smooth running of the Anglo-Norman state for what must have seemed to them an
inconsequential principle. This does not necessarily im-
ply that they were hostile to reform. We tend, perhaps
to see the ecclesiastical history of the twelfth century too
much from the viewpoint of Anselm and Becket, to be
influenced too easily by the semi-hagiographical accounts
of Eadmer or John of Salisbury. We can easily forget
that those who did not subscribe in full to the novel
ideas of the Gregorian reform might be adequate, even
admirable, bishops when judged by other standards.
Osmund of Salisbury (1078-99), for example, royal chancellor before his elevation, enjoyed a reputation for sanctity and was eventually canonised,[54] and even the notori-

---

54 D.H. Farmer, *The Oxford Dictionary of Saints*, Oxford 1978,
303-4.

ous Ranulf Flambard (1099-1128), instigator of Rufus's ecclesiastical policy, was remembered with great affection by the monks of his cathedral church of Durham.[55]

The majority of bishops, then, were drawn by background and circumspection towards the royal interpretation of the correct relationship between the secular power and the church. Most revealing of all, however, is the attitude adopted by William of St. Calais, bishop of Durham. In 1088, arraigned on a charge of treason, he had attempted to appeal to the pope; reconciled to the king, he was at Rockingham Rufus's main spokesman, and castigated Anselm for his recognition of Pope Urban II without royal permission. In fact, even those bishops who were not bound to the king by ties of service had a rather different view of papal authority to that cherished at Rome. For them the papacy was a jurisdictional institution to be utilised when circumstances were propitious, to be denied when it threatened their own position or when it meddled overmuch in the complexities of feudal government.

The church in England, as in any other province of western Europe, seldom presented a united front. The papacy might envisage a great universal corporation acknowledging the leadership of Rome, in which national and feudal divisions were a mere administrative convenience. In practice, local and particular interests tended to prevail. The unity of the church in England was disfigured throughout the twelfth century and beyond by

---

55 R.W. Southern, 'Ranulf Flambard', in his *Medieval Humanism and Other Studies*, Oxford 1970, 204.

the bitter dispute over the primacy between Canterbury and York.[56] During Henry I's reign Bishop Urban of Llandaff spent the greater part of his episcopate of twenty-six years protesting and appealing against the alleged territorial incursions of his fellow-bishops of Hereford and St. Davids.[57] The early twelfth century witnessed the growth of tension between the secular clergy and the monks; in 1123 the suffragan bishops of the province of Canterbury were prepared to go to almost any lengths to prevent the election of another Benedictine to the chair of St. Augustine.[58] The great religious houses, wealthy and influential societies such as St. Albans and Bury St. Edmunds, were engaged in a perpetual struggle to free themselves from the jurisdiction, which they saw as domination, of diocesan bishops. Monasteries founded in close proximity quarrelled and litigated about the boundaries of their estates, secular priests competed for the choicest benefices. In all these conflicts churchmen were prepared to utilise whichever jurisdiction promised the best results, that of king or pope, and sought as far as possible to reject either when it failed to deliver a favourable verdict.

It has traditionally been thought that the Conqueror and his sons did everything possible to impede access to the papal curia, and that they erected around their dominions

56 D. Nicholl, *Thurstan, Archbishop of York*, York 1964, chapters 2-4; D. Bethell, 'William of Corbeil and the Canterbury-York Dispute', *Journal of Ecclesiastical History* 19, 1968, 145-59.

57 M. Brett, *The English Church under Henry I*, 52-5.

58 D. Bethell, 'English Black Monks and Episcopal Elections in the 1120s', *English Historical Review* 84, 1969, 673-98.

a 'ring-fence' or barrier which would prevent both the entry of papal legates and the exit of potential litigants bound for Rome.[59] The Anglo-Norman rulers were most certainly determined to resist papal jurisdictional claims when these presented a threat to their ancient rights as duke or king, or to the stability of the realm. When in 1082 Odo of Bayeux was accused of treason against his half-brother the king, he claimed that as a bishop he might be tried only by the pope. The reply, given by Lanfranc (and repeated in 1088 to William of St. Calais), was that he was accused not as an ecclesiastic but as a tenant-in-chief, who was answerable in the *curia regis*. A far weaker king, Stephen, unsuccessfully forbade Archbishop Theobald to attend the papal council of Rheims in 1148, nominating three representatives of the entire English episcopate.[60] Throughout the period papal legates were allowed access to the kingdom only after long delays and to operate within parameters established by the king himself.

The various divisions and disputes within the English church, however, encouraged ecclesiastics to look to Rome for privileges which would safeguard the rights of their own sees or communities, and even for favourable judicial decisions.[61] And when the interests of the crown were not directly affected, recourse to the papal court

---

59 The classic statement of this thesis is Z.N. Brooke, *The English Church and the Papacy from the Conquest to the Reign of John*, Cambridge 1931, especially chapter 9.

60 R.H.C. Davis, *King Stephen*, 3rd edn 1990, 101-2.

61 An excellent survey of Anglo-papal relations, on which the following is based, is Brett, *English Church under Henry I*, chapter 2.

was not hindered as a matter of principle. Henry I never attempted to impede the continual appeals of Bishop Urban of Llandaff, since royal rights were in no way jeopardised by his internecine ecclesiastical quarrel; and despite a great deal of blustering by the king, the parties to the interminable primacy dispute between Canterbury and York eventually argued their cases in the papal curia, since northern separatism no longer presented the threat that it had in the Conqueror's reign. The resistance to papal legations came as much from Canterbury as from the king, for the archbishop habitually, and sometimes successfully, sought to exercise this office himself. In 1124, however, John of Crema was permitted by Henry I to fulfil this function, conducting a visitation of every bishopric and major abbey in England and in September 1125 presiding over a legatine council at Westminster. This was the first time since 1070 that a representative sent directly from Rome was able to exercise any real authority in England, and the legation made a great impression on contemporary writers.

Voluntary recourse to Rome was, however, more significant than legatine authority in accustoming English ecclesiastics to contact with the apostolic see. Papal justice increased in scope and volume in the course of the twelfth century for the same reasons as royal justice expanded under Henry I and Henry II. The exercise of centralised jurisdiction was an expression of authority, a prime factor in the creation of a united kingdom or a united Christendom, and justice to both popes and princes was a great source of profit. Rulers actively sought to increase their jurisdiction, but they were able to do so effectively only because of consumer demand. The science of canon law was in its infancy, the machinery for establishing the truth of allegations was rudimentary, but despite the difficulties caused by distance and by the subterfuge of litigants there was a marked tendency by 1135 to look to Rome as the ultimate tribunal in certain spheres of ecclesiastical justice. In 1100 the number of prelates known to have visited Rome can be counted on the fingers of one hand; by the end of Henry I's reign twelve out of fourteen bishops, nine of the greater abbots and a host of lesser clergy had made the journey, either on embassies or to participate in one of the *causes célèbres* of the reign. The episcopate and higher clergy were in the 1130s in no sense papalist, as against royalist, but even those bishops who had served their apprenticeship in the royal service recognised, as their predecessors fifty years before had not, that there were defined areas of ecclesiastical and religious life in which decisions were beyond royal competence. The king was no longer sacerdotal - that is, he was no longer regarded as God's deputy ruling over a unitary society in which there was no distinction between spiritual and temporal. The priestly function of kingship had been demolished by the Gregorian reform movement, and if in compensation the Anglo-Norman monarchy had created a superb administrative machine which retained control over the temporal aspects of the church, even as assertive a ruler as Henry I did not attempt to maintain or implement the old-fashioned (and theologically unsound) doctrines of the Anglo-Norman Anonymous, who had argued in desperation that the king represented the divinity of Christ, the priest merely His humanity.[62]

---

62 E.H. Kantorowicz, *The King's Two Bodies: a Study in Medieval Political Theology*, Princeton 1957, 42-60.

The Secular Aristocracy and Reform

Many historians, under the influence of contemporary monastic chroniclers, have viewed the western European aristocracy as enemies of reform, determined in general to maintain their stranglehold over the rich resources of the church. The two centuries before the Gregorian reform, indeed, have been described by two French experts as 'the church at the mercy of the laity'.[63] Yet in no region would the reform movement have made any progress without the support of a substantial number of lay lords.[64] It was the upper echelons of the laity who led the way in the lavish endowment of the church in Normandy and England in the late eleventh and early twelfth centuries, and it was from these ranks that the ecclesiastical hierarchy, not to mention the great majority of choir monks, were recruited.[65]

There was, of course, a lamentable record of depredation. Many of the 'new aristocracy' of Normandy carved out their position, in part at least, by the annexation in the 1040s of monastic estates; in the immediate post-

---

[63] E. Amann and A. Dumas, *L'Église au pouvoir des Laïques, 888-1057*, Paris 1948.

[64] For an important survey, see J. Howe, 'The Nobility's Reform of the Medieval Church', *American Historical Review* 93, 1988, 317-39; for a case study, J.C. Ward, 'Fashions in Monastic Endowment: Foundations of the Clare Family, 1066-1314', *Journal of Ecclesiastical History* 32, 1981, 427-51.

[65] For a general view, C. Harper-Bill, 'The Piety of the Anglo-Norman Knightly Class', *Proceedings of the Battle Conference on Anglo-Norman Studies* ii, 1980, 63-77, (notes) 173-7.

Conquest years English houses did lose some land to their Norman neighbours, and again during the relative disorder of Stephen's reign they were vulnerable to the desperate acquisitiveness of powerful yet threatened lords seeking to compensate for losses elsewhere. The fortunes of the Montgomeries, made infamous by Orderic Vitalis as the type of aggressive feudal lordship, were based partially on the amputation of estates from Bernay, Fécamp and Jumièges, yet before 1066 Roger of Montgomery, now thoroughly established, was a benefactor of St. Stephen's Caen, St. Evroult and, outside the duchy, of Cluny; thereafter he founded St. Nicholas Arundel as a dependency of his family monastery at Séez, established Shrewsbury as an independent abbey and refounded Much Wenlock, centre of the Anglo-Saxon cult of St. Milburga, as a Cluniac priory.[66] William de Warenne, Richard FitzGilbert of Clare and Picot the sheriff of Cambridgeshire were all regarded by the monks of Ely as rapacious enemies; viewed otherwise, they were the pious founders of houses in the vanguard of reform, respectively Cluniac, of the affiliation of Bec and Augustinian.[67] In a later generation Roger de Mowbray during the 'anarchy' made inroads on the estates of York minster, but he was a benefactor, albeit at a price, to the new Cistercian abbeys of Byland and Rievaulx and to

---

[66] For a reassessment of the family, see J.F.A. Mason, 'Roger of Montgomery and his Sons (1067-1102)', *Transactions of Royal Historical Society* 5th series 13, 1963, 1-28.

[67] E.O. Blake, ed., *Liber Eliensis*, Camden 3rd series 92, 1962, 188-9, 202-3, 210-12; Knowles and Hadcock, *Medieval Religious Houses*, 75, 92, 98, 100, 146.

other northern houses.[68] At the lower end of the scale of donation stands Roger de Clinton, one of Henry I's most rapacious agents, who established an Augustinian community at Kenilworth in 1125 with property almost entirely misappropriated from others through legal chicanery;[69] at the higher end David king of Scots, son of an Anglo-Saxon princess and lord of a great English honour, has been termed 'a connoisseur of the religious orders' who revolutionised the church in his northern kingdom by the sponsorship of reforming religious congregations.[70]

The reason for this torrent of patronage was undoubtedly the conviction that the monastic order represented the ideal and the yardstick of Christian observance, and that the prayers of the monks for their founders and benefactors would ease their path to salvation. The early medieval church constantly emphasised the desirability of peace and condemned aggression - a penance was imposed on all those who had fought with William at Hastings, although the duke's campaign had been sanctioned by the papacy,[71] and it was not until after the First Crusade that

68 D.E. Greenway, ed., *Charters of the Honour of Mowbray, 1107-91*, Oxford 1972, nos 32-69, 117-48, 318, 322.

69 R.W. Southern, 'King Henry I', in his *Medieval Humanism and Other Studies*, Oxford 1970, 216-17.

70 C.N.L. Brooke, 'King David I of Scotland as a Connoisseur of the Religious Orders', in C.E. Viola, ed., *Medievalia Christiana, xi*^e-*xiii*^e *siècles: Hommage à Raymonde Foreville*, Paris 1989, 320-34.

71 H.E.J. Cowdrey, 'Ermenfrid of Sion and the Penitential Ordinance following the Battle of Hastings', *Journal of Ecclesiastical History* 20, 1969, 225-42.

knighthood, if practised in accordance with religious precepts, came to be regarded as a laudable vocation.[72] Princes, lords and knights therefore ardently desired to share in the spiritual benefits of monasticism. Many actually entered the cloister, if only on their deathbeds; most made gifts, according to their means, to the religious, in return for their prayers and eventual burial within their precincts. There was nothing remotely cynical in this. Violence was at the same time essential for survival in this harsh competitive world, yet because of the church's strictures was deeply regretted. The monks were regarded as the knights of Christ, fighting the most important of all battles, against the Devil for men's souls, and long before William of Malmesbury described the new Cistercian order as 'the surest road to heaven',[73] the long-established Benedictines had been regarded in the same light. Whereas the young Anselm, travelling northwards from Italy in search of a monastic home, would not be professed at Cluny because the constant round of masses allowed no time for study or contemplation,[74] it was precisely this incessant liturgy which appealed to the Norman warrior-lord William de Warenne, who after his visit founded the first Cluniac priory in England at Lewes in 1077.[75]

---

72 C. Morris, '*Equestris Ordo*: Chivalry as a Vocation in the Twelfth Century', *Studies in Church History* 15, 1978, 87-96.

73 *English Historical Documents ii, 1042-1189*, 694.

74 R.W. Southern, ed., *The Life of St Anselm, Archbishop of Canterbury, by Eadmer*, Oxford 1962, 9.

75 Golding, 'The Coming of the Cluniacs', 65.

Over the next fifty years new forms of religious life evolved, breaking the Benedictine monopoly and challenging Cluny for the pinnacle of Christian observance.[76] Yet it was surely the same motivation which led Walter Espec, one of the greatest magnates of northern England in the 1130s, to found a house of Augustinian canons at Kirkham and a Cistercian community at Rievaulx.[77] From the late eleventh century to 1154 over ninety Augustinian houses were established in England and Wales, and from 1128 to 1152, when an ineffective ban on further expansion was imposed by the order's general chapter, over forty Cistercian foundations. In addition there were numerous nunneries, including nine communities of Gilbertines, the only native English congregation. The military orders, the Templars and Hospitallers, had recently established their first English depots to further their war-effort in the crusading states. These new houses were generally far less well-endowed than the long-established Benedictine monasteries, but on the other hand their estates were seldom burdened with knight service, and their foundation *en masse* represents a quite remarkable investment by all levels of society, but primarily by the aristocracy and the knightly class.

The Church's Ministry

In that aspect of the church's organisation which most

76 For the European context, see most conveniently J. Burton, 'Monastic Movements of the Eleventh and Twelfth Centuries', *Medieval History* I ii, 1991, 23-36.

77 Knowles and Hadcock, *Medieval Religious Houses*, 124, 162.

closely touched the religious life of the English people as a whole, the provision of convenient sites of worship, continental influence, either Norman or Gregorian, had little direct effect. From the late tenth to the mid-twelfth centuries there was a tremendous proliferation of small, local churches in England.[78] This multiplication was one important aspect of the transformation of society as a whole. In the century and a half before 1066 there emerged a broadly-based class of thegns, who exercised, each in a very limited area, many of the rights formerly reserved to king and great nobles. At the same time there was a steady development of village communities, the result of population growth and improving agricultural techniques. 'As with villages and field, so with the local church: there is probably no time at which it developed so rapidly and decisively as during the period between 1000 and 1150, for which the Domesday survey is the half-way mark.'[79]

Towards the end of the tenth century the predominant agency of pastoral care in England was the minster, a large church often sited in a royal manor, to which the population of an extensive area would come at great festivals, from which itinerant priests would venture forth to take the sacraments to outlying hamlets. This struc-

---

78 For what follows, see J. Blair, ed., *Minsters and Parish Churches: the Local Church in Transition, 950-1200*, Oxford University Committee for Archaeology Monograph 17, Oxford 1988, especially Blair's introduction; J. Blair, 'Local Churches in Domesday Book and Before', in J.C. Holt, ed., *Domesday Studies*, Woodbridge 1986, 265-78.

79 Blair, 'Local Churches in Domesday Book and Before', 265-6.

ture had been ideally suited to the missionary age - that of the initial conversion of the seventh century, or the period of reconversion after the first wave of Viking invasions. It used to be thought that the minsters suffered irreparably from these Scandinavian raids, but the few surviving tenth-century wills suggest that they remained at least until the 970s the normal focus of religious allegiance. Thereafter there was a building-boom in these mother churches between c. 975 and 1080. Similar institutions, indeed, were founded on the eve of the Conquest, by Earl Aelfric at Clare in Suffolk around 1045 and by Harold Godwineson at Waltham Holy Cross in 1060.[80]

From the late tenth century, however, there was a marked shift of endowment towards small local churches. Some of these were established by the clergy of the minsters, one of whose priests might take up semi-permanent residence in a large centre of population within its extended parish. Others were founded by lords of manors, sometimes without reference and in opposition to the minster clergy, whose revenues and influence were thereby threatened. In the villages of East Anglia there are indications of communal initiative, with the inhabitants themselves combining to establish their own church. Such corporate effort was certainly the norm in the expanding towns of eleventh-century England.

Domesday Book is not uniform in its listing of village churches, but of the better documented areas, Suffolk in

---

[80] J. Blair, 'Secular Minster Churches in Domesday Book', in P. Sawyer, ed., *Domesday Book: a Reassessment*, 1985, 104-42.

1086 had 345 churches for 639 sites of population and Huntingdonshire fifty-three churches for eighty-three places named.[81] For Kent, Domesday lists only 175 churches, whereas it has been demonstrated that within a generation of the Conquest there were in fact at least 400.[82] By the beginning of the thirteenth century London had ninety-nine parish churches and Winchester fifty-seven; most of these had been established by *c.* 1150.[83] Between the tenth and twelfth centuries twelve churches were founded within a mile along the main road running through the small town of Cambridge.[84] The rural parishes varied greatly in size, those in towns were almost uniformly small - the average size in London was three and a half acres. This proliferation of small parish churches, most especially in towns, is not paralleled elsewhere in northern Europe, and the contrast with Italy is especially marked, for in the peninsula, while there were numerous private chapels, all babies from city and region were received into the faith not in a local church, but in a great baptistery such as those still standing in Florence and Pisa.

---

81 R. Lennard, *Rural England, 1086-1135*, Oxford 1959, chapter 10 'The Village Churches', 288.

82 Blair, ed., *Minsters and Parish Churches*, 105.

83 C.N.L. Brooke and G. Keir, *London 800-1216: the Shaping of a City*, 1975, chapter 6 'On Parishes'; M. Biddle, ed., *Winchester in the Early Middle Ages: an Edition and Discussion of the Winton Domesday*, Oxford 1974, 329-36.

84 C.N.L. Brooke, 'The Churches of Medieval Cambridge', in D. Beales and G. Best, eds., *History, Society and the Churches: Essays in honour of Owen Chadwick*, Cambridge 1985, 49-76, at p.50.

For a century after 1050 there was a tremendous upsurge
in church building. Literally thousands of stone churches,
at first very simple in form and style, by the mid-twelfth
century increasingly sophisticated, rose all over England.
In the diocese of Canterbury, for example, in the fifty
years after Lanfranc became archbishop almost every
church was rebuilt and numerous new ones constructed,
while Bishop Wulfstan was noted by his biographer to
have dedicated numerous churches in Worcestershire and
Gloucestershire. These newly permanent churches were
given landed endowments, varying tremendously in extent but at least sufficient to provide sustenance for the
village priest, who was becoming a normal member of
every scattered rural community.

The old minsters, in many cases converted in the late
eleventh century into houses of Augustinian canons, at
first clung tenaciously to their ancient rights; yet if they
succeeded in retaining, often for centuries, financial interests in the new parish churches, and particularly in bur-
ial-dues, the bishops of the early twelfth century were
universally convinced that every community was entitled
to its own church. They never sought to suppress these
new centres of worship and pastoral care. From the time
of William Rufus, moreover, the minster clergy themselves increasingly recognised the realities of the new
world by splitting their own territories into small parishes, centred on local churches in which one of their
number had a personal financial interest.

By 1150, then, the English parochial system, of which
the most obvious evidence is the multitude of medieval
churches standing to this day all over England, had al-

ready in large measure been created by the joint efforts
of Anglo-Saxon and Anglo-Scandinavian communities
and new Norman lords, with the approval and often the
cooperation of the bishops. In this endeavour at least all
were united. The results of this proliferation of small,
intimate parochial units were, in the long term, almost
entirely beneficial. The close relationship between priest
and people which resulted was surely a prime factor in
the absence of those heresies which by the late twelfth
century were endemic throughout much of continental
Europe. Yet from the viewpoint of the reformed papacy
there were dangerous drawbacks to this multiplication of
independent parishes.

First, there was the risk that priests thoroughly integrated into their local communities, but isolated from
centres of reforming activity, would continue, as had
their predecessors in England and Normandy, to cohabit
with women whom they regarded as wives. It is obvious that in the countryside of England Lanfranc's conciliar decree of 1075, that no married man should henceforth be ordained and that no priest should take a new
wife, had little effect. In 1102 Archbishop Anselm took
a harder line, demanding that all clerical 'marriage' should
cease forthwith, and specifically ordering Bishop Herbert of Norwich to eject from their churches all priests
who kept women. The bishop was more realistic in his
view, that such dramatic action would leave his diocese
devoid of pastoral care.[85] It was almost inevitable that
married priests would seek to pass their churches on to
their sons, and in England hereditary right to ecclesiasti-

---

85 Brett, *English Church under Henry I*, 219

cal livings was openly acknowledged a century and more after the initiation of the great campaign for clerical celibacy. Around 1150 the bishop of Norwich referred openly and without obvious disapproval to the custom of that city by which a parson held a church as had his ancestors, and in the same diocese monastic patrons, who had been envisaged as the guardians of reform, were prepared to condone the successions of sons to fathers in their parish churches.[86] Similar cases have been revealed on the other side of the country, in the diocese of Hereford, and were doubtless common elsewhere.[87] Not until the thirteenth century, at the earliest, was the battle against clerical 'immorality' won in the English parishes. Interestingly, however, there is no evidence of popular outcry against married priests, as there was on the continent, often orchestrated by the papacy itself.[88] Rather in England Henry I, and later John, cynically sought to exploit the situation by fining those priests found guilty of incontinence.[89]

The second, and perhaps more serious, danger to reforming ideology was the strong possibility of lay domina-

---

86 C. Harper-Bill, 'The Struggle for Benefices in Twelfth-Century East Anglia', *Anglo-Norman Studies* xi, 1989, 113-32, especially 126-8.

87 B.R. Kemp, 'Hereditary Benefices in the Medieval English Church: a Herefordshire Example', *Bulletin of Institute of Historical Research* 43, 1970, 1-15; J. Barrow, 'Hereford Bishops and Married Clergy, *c.* 1130-1240', ibid. 60, 1987, 1-8.

88 R.I. Moore, *The Origins of European Dissent*, 1977, chapter 3 'The Crisis of Reform', especially pp. 62-3.

89 Brett, *English Church under Henry I*, 220 n.1.

tion and exploitation of small local churches. Historians have quite naturally focused primarily upon the great struggle of the papacy against emperors and kings for the freedom of the church at the highest level; but equally obnoxious was the local stranglehold of nobles and knights upon churches established by their ancestors on their estates. From the time of the Conquest, and increasingly in the first half of the twelfth century, lay rights in and profit from the proprietorship of churches were diminished. Ownership was gradually reduced to mere patronage, the right to nominate a priest, who must be suitable, to the bishop.[90] Once the rapidly evolving canon law and respectable public opinion rendered it impossible for lay lords to receive tithes and spiritual offerings, there emerged an increasing tendency to grant parish churches to monasteries. Materially much less was lost than by the gift of estates, spiritually the same dividend was acquired. Reformers sincerely believed that the transfer of local churches to monastic proprietorship would be a guarantee of their freedom. But the law of the church as much as the law of England treated a church as a piece of real estate, in which property rights transcended spiritual obligations. By the 1150s some monastic houses had already embarked upon a programme of financial exploitation designed to strip their parish churches of a great part of their revenues; such calculating policies were to become the norm in the second half of the century.[91] A new form of proprietary church was

---

90 B.R. Kemp, 'Monastic Possession of Parish Churches in the Twelfth Century', *Journal of Ecclesiastical History* 31, 1980, 133-59.
91 For an example, C. Harper-Bill, 'Battle Abbey and its East Anglian Churches', in C. Harper-Bill, C. Holdsworth and J.L. Nelson, eds., *Studies in Medieval History presented to R. Allen Brown*, Woodbridge 1989, 159-72.

created alongside the relics of the old.

The Reign of Stephen

The reign of King Stephen has conventionally been seen as a watershed in the history of the English church. It has been argued that now at last, with the breakdown of royal authority, the barrier erected by the Conqueror was breached, the English church for the first time enjoyed free intercourse with Rome and leading ecclesiastics absorbed novel views of the nature of Christian society which made them unwilling to submit any longer to royal control as it had previously been exercised.[92] Stephen, of course, was in a weaker position than his predecessors because there was an active and feasible rival claimant for his throne.[93] The concessions which he made to the church in the Oxford charter of liberties of April 1136 were more specific than those of Henry I's coronation charter, and there was greater expectation that he might be held to them. His arrest of Bishop Roger of Salisbury and his episcopal nephews in 1139 prompted a reaction, spearheaded by the king's brother Henry of Blois, bishop of Winchester and papal legate, which would have been unthinkable when Odo of Bayeux and William of St. Calais had been imprisoned half a century earlier. When the two brothers, now reconciled, attempted to advance their nephew William FitzHerbert to the archbishopric of York, the norther Cistercians invoked the outraged fury of St. Bernard of Clairvaux, who prevailed

---

92 Z.N. Brooke, *The English Church and the Papacy*, 175-90.

93 H.A. Cronne, *The Reign of Stephen*, 1970, chapter 4 'Stephen, Henry of Blois and the Church'; R.H.C. Davis, *King Stephen*, passim.

upon a Cistercian pope to quash the appointment.[94] For the first time in Stephen's reign there are indications of free elections to bishoprics, as at Norwich in 1144, and the see of Hereford was filled by agreement between pope and archbishop of Canterbury, who towards the end of the reign prevented the creation of a dynasty by their refusal to sanction the succession of Stephen's son.

It would be a fair judgement that Stephen's reign did not so much mark a watershed in the relationship between pope, king and English church, but rather that his problems and his need for ecclesiastical support accelerated the development of trends already apparent before 1135.[95] The chronicler Henry of Huntingdon believed, for example, that it was in the early years of the reign, during the legateship of Henry of Blois (1139-43), that appeals were first made to Rome. This is not the case, for they had occurred under Henry I, but they now became far more frequent, and for the first time there is evidence of native ecclesiastical judges on the spot being commissioned by the pope to hear cases in England, administering a legal code which had achieved a new level of definition, albeit provisional, with the publication in 1140 of Gratian's *Concordance of Discordant Canons* (or *Decretum*), which provided the basis for the Romanisation and the rationalisation of the law of the church.[96] Eng-

---

94 M.D. Knowles, 'The Case of St William of York', in his *The Historian and Character*, Cambridge 1963, 76-97.

95 Duggan, 'From the Conquest to the Reign of John', 84-7.

96 For early papal judges-delegate, see various cases in W.J. Millor and H.E. Butler, eds., *The Letters of John of Salisbury* i, *The Early Letters*, 1955; for Gratian, see Morris, *The Papal Monarchy*, 400-3, 575-6.

lishmen at this crucial time became prominent in the papal curia - Robert Pullen became chancellor of the Roman church in 1144, and ten years later Cardinal Nicholas Breakspeare was elected as the only (to date) English pope, Adrian IV. Legatine authority in England became more pervasive than it had ever been before, whether exercised by special emissaries from the popes such as Alberic of Ostia in 1138-9 or by the king's brother. The strength of the English church in the mid-twelfth century is perhaps symbolised by the contrast between Henry of Blois, the prince-bishop, and Theobald, abbot of Bec, who in January 1139 became archbishop of Canterbury.[97] Henry was determined that not even his own brother should trample underfoot the liberties of the church, Theobald less dramatically struggled to hold together his ecclesiastical province within a divided kingdom. Both of them looked to Rome for support and thus consolidated and perpetuated English participation in that expansion of papal jurisdiction which was a noteworthy feature of western European history in the first half of the twelfth century. Both Henry and Theobald recognised by 1154, however, that political weakness did not further the church's pastoral mission, and both were instrumental in the creation of that balance of power in the affairs of the English church which was only briefly interrupted by Becket's stand against Henry II.

---

97 For Theobald, see A. Saltman, *Theobald, Archbishop of Canterbury*, 1955, repr. New York 1969. A new biography of Henry of Blois is promised by M.J. Franklin.

Conclusion

The main lines of development of the English church
had, in fact, become clear by the death of Henry I in
1135. The lavish endowment of monasticism, which
had been interrupted in the early eleventh century, had
been resumed by the new Norman lords of the land, who
both took to their hearts the ancient Benedictine foundations and were instrumental in the plantation of new
communities of continental origin and diverse character-
istics. These new orders soon attracted donations and
recruits from surviving native landholders. The steady
multiplication of parish churches, initiated by Old English lords and communities, continued unabated and was
fostered by the Norman newcomers, although in all but
the most richly endowed local churches the village priest
was likely to be of Anglo-Saxon or Scandinavian de-
scent. The status of the clerical order had in theory been
raised by the Gregorian ideology, but in most English
parishes the close affinity of priest and people was probably not affected. The higher clergy, on the other hand,
were separated from their subordinates and from the people
both by their racial origin (although by the mid-twelfth
century the difference between French and English was
already beginning to become blurred) and by the triumph
of the ideal of celibacy. They had, moreover, become
accustomed to contact with Rome, without believing that
such links in any way diminished the role of a formi-
dable king who, if he had abandoned the image of sacral
kingship and surrendered the empty symbolism of investiture, retained real control over the personnel and estates of the church.

SELECT BIBLIOGRAPHY

In the following bibliography, articles to which reference is made in footnotes are not normally here listed again.

Sources

A large number of contemporary sources are available in translation, most notably in the series of Oxford (formerly Nelson's) Medieval Texts. Most relevant to ecclesiastical history in that series are:

M. Chibnall, ed., *The Ecclesiastical History of Orderic Vitalis*, 6 vols, Oxford 1969-80.

H. Clover and M. Gibson, eds., *The Letters of Lanfranc, Archbishop of Canterbury*, Oxford 1979.

M.D. Knowles, ed., *The Monastic Constitutions of Lanfranc*, 1951.

H.E.J. Cowdrey, ed., *The* Epistolae Vagantes *of Pope Gregory VII*, Oxford 1972, especially nos. 1, 16, 34, 57.

R.W. Southern, ed., *The Life of St. Anselm, Archbishop of Canterbury, by Eadmer*, Oxford 1962.

C. Johnson, ed., *Hugh the Chantor: the History of the Church of York, 1066-1127*, revised edn. 1990 by M. Brett, C.N.L. Brooke and M. Winterbottom.

C.H. Talbot, *The Life of Christina of Markyate*, Oxford 1959.

M. Chibnall, ed., *The* Historia Pontificalis of *John of Salisbury*, 1956.

R. Foreville and G. Keir, eds., *The Book of St. Gilbert*, Oxford 1987.

Other modern translations available are:

S. Vaughn, *The Abbey of Bec and the Anglo-Norman State*, Woodbridge 1981 (contains the Life of Herluin and other Bec texts).

E. Emerton, *The Correspondence of Pope Gregory VII*, New York 1932 (Columbia University paperback reprint 1991), especially pp. 19-21, 30-2, 107-9, 114-6, 154-6, 182-3.

G. Bosanquet, *Eadmer's History of Recent Events in England*, 1964.

The Nuns of Malling, *The Life of Gundulf*, Malling Abbey 1968.

William of Malmesbury's *History of the Kings of England* and Simeon of Durham's *History of the Kings of England* and *History of the Church of Durham* are available in facsimile reprints of the nineteenth-century translation by Joseph Stephenson from Llanerch Enterprises, Lampeter.

The conciliar legislation of the English church is collected in D. Whitelock, M. Brett and C.N.L. Brooke, eds., *Councils and Synods, with Other Documents relating to the English Church* i, *A.D. 871-1204*, part 2, *1066-1204*, Oxford 1981. The texts are in Latin, but there are synopses and important discussion. Also in Latin but with English synopses are the various volumes of the British Academy series *English Episcopal Acta*, which print all known documents issued by the English bishops; relevant volumes already published are: i, *Lincoln 1067-1185*, ed. D.M. Smith, 1980; v, *York 1070-1154*, ed. J.E. Burton, 1988; vi, *Norwich 1070-1214*, ed. C. Harper-Bill, 1990.

A convenient selection of documents in translation is in D.C. Douglas and G.W. Greenaway, eds., *English Historical Documents* ii, *1042-1189*, 1968, especially pp. 587-694.

For important discussion of the sources, see A. Gransden, *Historical Writing in England, c. 550-c. 1307*, 1974, chapters 5-10.

Continental Religious and Ecclesiastical Background

B. Hamilton, *Religion in the Medieval West*, 1986.

C. Morris, *The Papal Monarchy: the Western Church from 1050-1250*, Oxford 1989.

I.S. Robinson, *The Papacy 1073-1198: Continuity and Innovation*, Cambridge 1990.

R.W. Southern, *Western Society and the Church in the Middle Ages*, Harmondsworth 1970.

B. Tierney, *The Crisis of Church and State, 1050-1300*, Englewood Cliffs 1964.

General Studies

For the last phase of the Old-English church, see:

F. Barlow, *The English Church 1000-1066: a Constitutional History*, 1963.

R.R. Darlington, 'Ecclesiastical Reform in the Later Old-English Period', *English Historical Review* 51, 1936, 385-428.

M. Deanesly, *The Pre-Conquest Church in England*, 1961, chapters 12-15.

C.J. Godfrey, *The Church in Anglo-Saxon England*, Cambridge 1962, chapters 18-24.

Important studies of the Anglo-Norman church are:

F. Barlow, *The English Church, 1066-1154*, 1979.

M. Brett, *The English Church under Henry I*, Oxford 1975.

Z.N. Brooke, *The English Church and the Papacy from*

the Conquest to the Reign of John, Cambridge 1931.

Biographical Studies

M. Gibson, *Lanfranc of Bec*, Oxford 1978.

E. Mason, *Wulfstan of Worcester*, Oxford 1990.

A. Gransden, 'Baldwin, Abbot of Bury St. Edmunds', *Anglo-Norman Studies* iv, 1982, 65-76.

J.W. Alexander, 'Herbert of Norwich, 1091-1119: Studies in the History of Norman England', *Studies in Medieval and Renaissance History* 6, 1969, 115-232.

R.W. Southern, *St Anselm and his Biographer*, Cambridge 1963.

R.W. Southern, *St Anselm: a Portrait in a Landscape*, Cambridge 1990.

S. Vaughn, *Anselm of Bec and Robert of Meulan: the Innocence of the Dove and the Wisdom of the Serpent*, Berkeley 1987.

E.J. Kealey, *Roger of Salisbury, Viceroy of England*, Berkeley 1972.

D. Nicholl, *Thurstan, Archbishop of York*, York 1964.

D. Bethell, 'William of Corbeil and the Canterbury-York Dispute', *Journal of Ecclesiastical History* 19, 1968, 145-59.

A.G. Dyson, 'The Monastic Patronage of Bishop Alexander of Lincoln', *Journal of Ecclesiastical History* 26, 1975, 1-24.

A. Saltman, *Theobald, Archbishop of Canterbury*, 1955, reprinted New York 1969.

A. Young, *William Cumin, Border Politics and the Bishopric of Durham, 1141-44*, Borthwick pamphlet 54, York 1978.

A. Morey and C.N.L. Brooke, *Gilbert Foliot and his Letters*, Cambridge 1965.

Monasticism

M.D. Knowles, *The Monastic Order in England*, Cambridge 1940.

D. Matthew, *The Norman Monasteries and their English Possessions*, Oxford 1962.

M. Chibnall, *The World of Orderic Vitalis*, Oxford 1984.

J.C. Dickinson, *The Origins of the Austin Canons and their Introduction into England*, 1950.

B.D. Hill, *English Cistercian Monasteries and their Patrons in the Twelfth Century*, Chicago 1968.

S. Thompson, *Women Religious: the Founding of English Nunneries after the Norman Conquest*, Oxford 1991.

For the monastic impact on the North of England, see:

L.G.D. Baker, 'The Desert in the North', *Northern History* 5, 1970, 1-11.

A. Dawtry, 'The Benedictine Revival in the North: the Last Bulwark of Anglo-Saxon Monasticism?', *Studies in Church History* 18, 1982, 87-98.

For various aspects, see M. Chibnall, 'Monks and Pastoral Work: a Problem in Anglo-Norman History', *Journal of Ecclesiastical History* 18, 1967, 165-71; T. Callahan, Jnr., 'The Impact of the Anarchy on English Monasticism, 1135-54', *Albion* 6, 1974, 219-32; C.J. Holdsworth, 'Ideas and Reality: Some Attempts to Control and Defuse War in the Twelfth Century', *Studies in Church History* 20, 1983, 59-78; C.J. Holdsworth, 'Orderic, Traditional Monk, and the New Monasticism', in D. Greenway, C. Holdsworth and J. Sayers, eds., *Tradition and Change: Essays in honour of Marjorie Chibnall*, Cambridge 1985, 21-34.

For a series of useful studies on the relationship between the laity and the church, see E. Mason, 'Timeo barones et dona ferentes', *Studies in Church History* 15, 1978, 61-76; 'A Truth Universally Acknowledged', ibid., 16, 1979, 171-86; '*Pro Statu et Incolumnitate Regni Mei*: Royal Monastic Patronage, 1066-1154', ibid., 18, 1982, 99-118.

There are numerous studies of the administration of individual ecclesiastical estates; among the best are:

F.R.H. Du Boulay, *The Lordship of Canterbury*, 1966.

B.F. Harvey, *Westminster Abbey and its Estates in the Middle Ages*, Oxford 1977.

E. King, *Peterborough Abbey, 1086-1310: a Study in the Land Market*, Cambridge 1973.

E. Miller, *The Abbey and Bishopric of Ely*, Cambridge 1951.

E. Searle, *Lordship and Community: Battle Abbey and its Banlieu, 1066-1538*, Toronto 1974.

The Anglo-Norman Church and its Immediate Neighbours

For want of space, this important topic has not been considered in this pamphlet, and I hope to deal with it elsewhere. For an excellent survey, of significance far beyond Ireland, see M.T. Flanagan, *Irish Society, Anglo-Norman Settlers, Angevin Kingship*, Oxford 1989, chapters 1-2; see also G.W.S. Barrow, *The Kingdom of the Scots*, 1973, chapters 5,6; C.N.L. Brooke, *The Church and the Welsh Border in the Central Middle Ages*, Woodbridge 1986; M. Richter, *Giraldus Cambrensis: the Growth of the Welsh Nation*, Aberystwyth 1976; J.A. Watt, *The Church and the Two Nations in Medieval Ireland*, Cambridge 1970, chapter 1.

CHRISTOPHER HARPER-BILL
BIBLIOGRAPHY

1977

'Bishop Richard Hill and the Court of Canterbury, 1494-96', *Guildhall Studies in London History* iii, 1-12.

'A Late Medieval Visitation: the Diocese of Norwich in 1499', *Proceedings of Suffolk Institute of Archaeology* xxxiv, 35-47.

'The Priory and Parish of Folkestone in the Fifteenth Century', *Archaeologia Cantiana* xciii, 195-200.

1978

'Archbishop John Morton and the Province of Canterbury, 1486-1500', *Journal of Ecclesiastical History* xxix, 1-21.

'Herluin Abbot of Bec and his Biographer', *Studies in Church History* xv, 15-25.

1979

'The *Familia*, Administrators and Patronage of Archbishop John Morton', *Journal of Religious History* x, 236-52.

1980 (-81)

The Cartulary of Blythburgh Priory, 2 vols, Suffolk Record Society.

'The Piety of the Anglo-Norman Knightly Class', *Proceedings of the Battle Conference on Anglo-Norman Studies* ii, 63-77, 173-6 (notes).

'Cistercian Visitation in the Late Middle Ages: the Case of Hailes Abbey', *Bulletin of the Institute of Historical Research* liii, 103-14.

1981
'Monastic Apostasy in Late Medieval England', *Journal of Ecclesiastical History* xxxii, 1-18.

1982 (-84)
with R. Mortimer, *The Stoke by Clare Cartulary*, 3 vols, Suffolk Record Society.

1983
'Church and Society in Twelfth-Century Suffolk: the Charter Evidence', *Proceedings of the Suffolk Institute of Archaeology* xxxv.

1985
'The Labourer is Worthy of his Hire?: Complaints about Diet in Late Medieval English Monasteries', in C.M. Barron and C. Harper-Bill, eds, *The Church in Pre-Reformation Society: Essays in Honour of F.R.H. DuBoulay*, Woodbridge, 95-107.

1987
The Register of John Morton, Archbishop of Canterbury, 1486-1500, vol. i, *Canterbury and York Society* lxxv.

1988
'Christianity in the West to the Reformation', in *The World's Religions*, ed. S.R. Sutherland *et al.*, London, 131-53.
'John Colet's Convocation Sermon and the Pre-Reformation Church in England' *History* lxxiii, 191-210.

1989

The Pre-Reformation Church in England, 1400-1530, Longman Seminar Studies in History.

'R. Allen Brown: a Personal Appreciation', and 'Battle Abbey and its East Anglian Churches', in C. Harper-Bill, C.J. Holdsworth and J.L. Nelson, eds, *Studies in Medieval History presented to R. Allen Brown*, Woodbridge, 1-5, 159-72.

'The Struggle for Benefices in Twelfth-Century East Anglia', *Anglo-Norman Studies*, xi, 113-32.

1990

English Episcopal Acta vi: Norwich 1070-1214, British Academy.

St Thomas of Canterbury, Canterbury Cathedral Gifts pamphlet.

'The Early History of the Church of Bacton', *Proceedings of the Suffolk Institute of Archaeology* xxxvii, 95-101.

1991

The Cartulary of the Augustinian Friars of Clare, Suffolk Record Society.

The Register of John Morton, Archbishop of Canterbury, 1486-1500, vol. ii, Canterbury and York Society lxxviii.

editor, *Religious Belief and Ecclesiastical Careers in Late Medieval England*, Woodbridge.

1992

'Who Wanted the English Reformation?', *Medieval History*, Vol. II no. 1.